My

Wisconsin

Journal

Pambling Roads

Books by Pamela Ackerson

The Wilderness Time Travel Series
Across the Wilderness
Into the Wilderness
Wilderness Bound
Warriors of the Wilderness
Out of the Wilderness
The Wilderness Series Ebook box set

Wounded Heroes Anthology (with Debra Parmley, Teri Riggs, Maggie Adams, and Nia Farrell)

PI Series Time Travel
The Gingerbread House
Garrett's Ghost
Living the Wright Life

Historical Fiction
Dear Margaret,

Non-fiction
I Was Just a Radioman (A memoir of a Pearl Harbor survivor, Black Cat, and decorated veteran.)
Be More Successful with Marketing and AdvertiZING
I am a Runner — the Memoirs of a Sepsis Survivor

A Granny Pants Story   (Children's Stories)
The Long and Little Doggie
Riley Gets into Predicaments
Available in Spanish:
El Perrito Largo y el Perrito Pequeno (La Serie del Perrito Largo y Pequeno)

Short Stories

The Clere Restaurant Collection
Sunday at 7
With a Side of Love
Winds from the Past
The Throuple with Love
The Best Catch of His Life

A Rosa for Russell ~ from the Wounded Heroes Anthology

Pambling Roads Journals —

Pages for you to fill in the blanks! Nurture your creativity with Pambling Roads State Journals, interactive journals designed to spark imagination and self-motivation. They include historical trivia and tidbits about each state, and a small section in the front of the book by the author sharing her travels.

States:

Alabama   Arizona   Arkansas   California   Colorado
Florida   Georgia   Idaho   Illinois   Indiana   Iowa
Kansas   Kentucky   Louisiana   Maine   Maryland
Massachusetts   Michigan   Minnesota   Mississippi
Missouri   Montana   Nebraska   Nevada   New Hampshire
New Mexico   New York   North Dakota   Oregon   Rhode
Island   South Carolina   South Dakota   Ohio   Oklahoma
Tennessee   Texas   Utah   Vermont   Virginia
Washington   Washington, D.C.

More to come! Check your favorite bookstore for the latest state journals.

Fortune Cookie Wisdom Journals

My Wisconsin Journal
Pambling Roads
Pamela Ackerson

Cover Design: Dora Gonzalez

PamelaAckerson.com
@PamAckerson
Pam@PamelaAckerson.com

Our travels have brought us all around the "lower 48". We've tried to zip zag, circle through, and around every state we could. Florida was where this endeavor started.

Enjoy your journal.

Thank you for taking this wonderful journey with us. It has been absolutely incredible.

Please keep in mind that some museums don't allow photography and will not be available on the Pambling Roads Blog

Pambling Roads—My Wisconsin Journal

Wisconsin

Welcome back and thank you for continuing to make this travel series a wonderful success. Pambling Roads continues as we travel up the center of the U.S. along the Mississippi River and over aiming for the mid-west states.

Madison

Wisconsin is up there on the top ten list of most beautiful states. The people were wonderful, friendly, and welcoming. It'll most likely be one of the states that we return to for a holiday.

House on the Rock

House on the Rock located in Spring Green Wisconsin, near Dodgeville. It started out as Alex Jordan's own personal resort and turned into a spectacular breathtaking home where he collected artifacts, relics, and displays to please his guests. The house was strategically built around the rocks, in the crevices, and on the cliff for a panoramic view of the countryside. The gardens were elaborately decorated with sculptures, waterfalls, flora, and fish in the lily pad filled ponds.

The Infinity Room stretches out like a futuristic anomaly, engineered to extend from the cliff for 218 feet and 156 feet above the ground.

We purchased a few things from the gift shop and some mint fudge. The employees from the moment we walked in the door until we left were all very pleasant and helpful.

Schurman's Wisconsin Cheese Country

We stopped at Schurman's Wisconsin Cheese Country and bought some cheese curds. We tried some and then sent the rest of the bag to our daughter since she loves cheese. We chatted a bit with the gentleman that works there. He was very courteous and friendly. We told him which direction we would be traveling and he recommended we visit Wyalusing State Park.

We tried visiting Little Norway but it was still closed for the season and may be closed permanently. Even though I have never seen it, there was disappointment that such a wonderful place wasn't open yet for visitors.

Their online gift shop is open for business if you are searching for unique gifts.

Wyalusing State Park

Wyalusing was wonderful. We are so glad we went to the park. We stopped at Point Lookout, which gives you a breathtaking view of the Mississippi and Wisconsin River. We drove over to the Green Cloud picnic area, walked near the Indian Mounds along the coastline of the river, and the monument for the Passenger Pigeons. The fee was $5 for an hour and was well worth the fee.

Prairie du Chien

We went to the Mississippi River, went to the park, and put our feet in the water.

We stayed at the Best Western in Prairie du Chien. The employees there were happy and very helpful. The pool and hot tub were so relaxing after a bumpy highway on our old bones and muscles. Prairie du Chien has a lot of history and if we had more time, we could have enjoyed their festival scheduled for the weekend.

Driving through Wisconsin, we noticed large quilt squares on some barn buildings. We asked about them and found the story fascinating. They are displayed to symbolize family, history, and traditions.

Fort Crawford

We visited Fort Crawford museum. Nancy welcomed us with a greeting and a smile. She answered our questions about the fort and the quilt squares we saw on the barns. She was very pleasant and helpful.

It is one of the chain of forts along the Mississippi River. There were some pretty influential names involved with the fort. The fort had to be relocated and Colonel Zachary Taylor directed the construction along with Lt. Jefferson Davis. Dr. William Beaumont, known for his research on the digestive system was a military post surgeon at the fort.

A portion of the wall is original and they restored and added a building to replicate the original existing hospital. It is the only Fort Crawford building still standing. Touring the two buildings you can learn about Prairie du Chien's history, military information, the battle of 1814, and very interesting medical history.

Villa Louis

The Villa Louis is an historical home of one of their prominent families. It is a nineteenth century Victorian home and ninety percent of the furnishings are original

Dousman family. We toured the guesthouse, which was also used as the Dousman's office and entertainment area. The main house was also part of the guided tour. There are fourteen buildings that go with this tour. Most are self-guided, many aren't open yet for viewing, however, the fur museum was open, and we found it quite fascinating.

On the property are also some archaeological remains of Fort Crawford.

We had dinner at Huckleberry's restaurant. The food was awesome. The service was great. They have an awesome gift shop so even if you aren't hungry; it is definitely worth shopping at and purchasing some great gifts.

Red granite is the state rock.

The robin is the state bird.

The badger is the state animal.

The wood violet is state flower.

The state tree is the sugar maple.

The state motto is *forward*.

Wisconsin has multiple nicknames, one is the Badger State.

Wisconsin is also called 'America's Dairy Land' because it's
leads in the production of dairy products.

Green Bay is the Toilet Paper Capital of the World.

There are over 14,000 lakes in Wisconsin.

Sauk City is the oldest incorporated village in the state.

There are over 1.5 million milk cows in Wisconsin.

Wisconsin was the first state to enact an income tax law.

Wausau is the Ginseng Capital of the World.

Sheboygan is the Bratwurst Capital of the World.

The American Birkebeiner, a 52K ski race, is the largest in North America.

The National Freshwater Fishing Hall of Fame is located in
Hayward.

Noah's Ark, the largest water park in the United States, is in
Wisconsin Dells.

Mt. Horeb is the Troll Capital of the World.

The Hamburger Hall of Fame is in Seymour.

Mount Horeb has a Mustard Museum with over 2300 different varieties of mustard on display.

Labor Day weekend, Prairie du Sac hosts the State Cow Chip Throwing Contest.

Eagle River is the Snowmobile Capital of the World.

Wisconsin produces more milk than any other state.

____

____

____

____

____

____

____

____

____

____

____

____

____

____

____

____

____

____

____

____

There are over 15,000 snowmobile trails in Wisconsin.

Bloomer is the Jump Rope Capital of the World.

Milwaukee's Summerfest is the largest music festival in the
United States.

At a little over 1950 feet, Timm's Hill near Ogema is the
highest point in the state.

EAA AirVenture Oshkosh is the largest air show circuit in the world.

The Milwaukee Art Museum is one of the largest in the United
States.

In 1655, Green Bay Trading Post was established.

In 1686, Fort St. Antoine was established.

In 1690, lead was found in Wisconsin.

In 1764, Green Bay became a permanent settlement.

In 1781, Prairie du Chien was established.

In 1795, a fur trading post was established in what is now called Milwaukee.

In 1814, Fort Shelby was built. (Fort Crawford)

In 1833, Green Bay Intelligencer began printing Wisconsin's first newspaper.

In 1844, the utopian colony Wisconsin Phalanx was established at Ripon.

In 1844, George Esterly, of Janesville, invented the first harvesting machine.

Founded in 1846, Beloit College is the oldest college in Wisconsin.

The first telegram was received in Milwaukee in 1848.

The Institute for Education of the Blind was opened in Janesville in 1850.

In 1854, the Republican Party was founded in Ripon.

In 1856, the Schurz family of Watertown, opened the first kindergarten in the United States.

In 1868, Christopher Sholes patented the first typewriter.

In 1873, John Kohler began manufacturing the world's first enameled cast iron plumbing fixtures.

The Wind Point Lighthouse was built in 1880 and is 112 feet above the lake level.

Between 1882, the first commercial hydroelectric plant opened in Appleton.

In 1884, the Ringling Brothers opened 'The World's Greatest Show' for the first time in Baraboo.

The first electric streetcar system opened in Appleton in 1886.

In 1911, Wisconsin passed the nation's first Workers Compensation Law.

WHA is the oldest radio station in the United States. (1915)

The first unemployment assistance/benefits in the United States was passed in Wisconsin in 1932.

In 1965, Wisconsin became the first state to pass discrimination laws.

In 1968, the first bone-marrow transplant was performed at the University of Wisconsin.

Waukesha is known for natural springs.

Birnamwood has the world's largest badger.

Cave of the Mounds is a limestone cave in Blue Mounds.

Kewaunee has the world's tallest grandfather clock.

Wisconsin Dells has the world's largest flamingo.

Two Rivers is the birthplace of the ice cream sundae.

Wisconsin has a little over 100 waterfalls.

Crystal Cave is the longest cave in Wisconsin.

The Kingdom of Talossa in Milwaukee is a sovereign nation
with an interesting history.

The world's largest six pack is located in La Crosse.

The Golden Rondelle is a spaceship shaped theater in Racine.

Milwaukee has a Bobblehead Hall of Fame and Museum.

Laona has the world's largest soup kettle.

Places of Note:

House on the Rock ~~ thehouseontherock.com

Schurman's Wisconsin Cheese Country ~~
SchurmansCheese.com

Barn Quilts ~~ GreenCountyBarnQuilts.com

Fort Crawford Museum ~~ FortCrawfordMuseum.com

Villa Louis ~~ VillaLouis.WisconsinHistory.org

Thank you for purchasing your wonderful journal so you could fill in the blanks!

It's been a great adventure for, meeting the Americans, and meeting people from all over the world. Don't forget to check out the other Pambling Road Journals.

They make wonderful gifts.

Have you been to any of the places I've mentioned? Do you have stories to tell as well? Visit the Pambling Roads Blogs and add in your comments.

PamelaAckerson.com
Twitter: @PamAckerson